Goodbye Me Hello Me

Goodbye Me Hello Me

**LETTING GO OF THE PAST,
TO EMBRACE THE FUTURE**

A journey of discovering and finding yourself again,
to live the best version of YOU

JENNIFER V M WILLIAMS

Goodbye Me, Hello Me
© 2019 Jennifer V M Williams

All rights reserved. This book or parts thereof may not be reproduced in any form, stored in any retrieval system, or transmitted in any form by any means—electronic, mechanical, photocopy, recording, or otherwise—without prior written permission of the publisher, except as provided by United Kingdom copyright law. For permission requests, contact the publisher at:

Jennifer V M Williams
Kemp House,
152 - 160 City Road,
London,
EC1V 2NX
United Kingdom

support@jvmwilliams.com
www.jvmwilliams.com

First Edition
ISBN: 978-1-9999971-1-3

Although the author and publisher have made every effort to ensure that the information in this book was correct at press time, the author and publisher do not assume and hereby disclaim any liability to any party for any loss, damage, or disruption caused by errors or omissions, whether such errors or omissions result from negligence, accident, or any other cause.

Cover & Interior Design, Richell Balansag. Editor, Brittany Lewis. Author Photograph, Prasad Siva.

~

*This book is dedicated to you.
May you find the freedom to be
yourself in this world, and discover
a life full of happiness as YOU.*

~

CONTENTS

Thank You.................................9
Preface..................................11
Introduction 17
ONE: Where It All Begins......................21
TWO: Help, I'm Stuck........................31
THREE: Goodbye 41
FOUR: Lost Property........................53
FIVE: Silence 63
SIX: Stop, Look and Listen......................73
SEVEN: Bite Size...........................85
EIGHT: Let's Go!...........................95
NINE: Say Hello............................107
TEN: Recap!.............................117
Conclusion 127
About the Author 139
Goodbye Me, Hello Me E-Course 141

THANK YOU

First, I want to thank Almighty God for His grace and love that has kept me strong in everything I have been through in life. Words don't do it justice to my depth of love and adoration that I am still here and standing against all odds.

To my family. Thank you for always being there for me, especially at my most difficult and vulnerable moments in life, and allowing the time and space that I needed to just be me. I love you all dearly from the bottom of my heart.

To my dearest friend Nataline Green. Words cannot begin to describe how much you mean to me, and for your love, support, friendship, and sisterhood over the years. Thank you for being there when it mattered most.

PREFACE

I wrote the book Goodbye Me, Hello Me because of where I saw myself in life at that moment in time. I was the person constantly looking in the mirror, and not being happy with what I saw. My life on the outside wasn't mirroring up and reflecting who I knew I was on the inside. That led to a build-up of frustration, sadness, and sometimes anger at myself, as if I had let myself down in some way. I wasn't living up to be the person I knew I could be, and the person I was created to be. I would get my measuring stick out, hold it up against other people and their lives, and that just made me feel even worse and more disappointed with myself. I felt lost, worthless, and sometimes, broken. I was over-whelmed by that feeling of not having any value, or anything significant to offer. My life just wasn't reflecting who I was on the inside. It felt like the real me was crying out from within, trying to get out. Crying for attention that I was not able to give it. There was a disconnect somewhere, and I had to figure out where, and the reason why. I would find myself speaking with people, especially those I knew, and they too felt like they were living a life as a different person. They were not happy in their job, career, with their finances, family, and so much more. So, I knew I wasn't the only one. I wasn't alone, and I felt a sigh of relief. There were times I felt like walking away. I just had to figure out if I was walking away from my life, or from myself.

So, what changed?

I had to take time out. Time away from everything and everyone to be with myself. I had to reconnect back to my core and my source to discover who I was again – my God-given identity, and to re-discover my calling in life, so I could walk out again with a purpose and a mission. I had to revisit my visions and dreams again, so that they could be awakened from slumber and become alive. I had to take time out from everything, and from nearly everyone, telling myself that it is okay to do so. I had to learn to put some things on hold and terminate some things that no longer served their purpose in my life. I stepped away from social media and friends, and spent a lot of time by myself, and with myself. I stepped away from the business I was doing at the time. I learned to be quiet and still, as my body had forced me to. I was battling with health issues, fatigue and burnout. I had to pay attention and listen to what my body needed, even if I did not like the answer.

I followed a lot of the steps and keys that I spoke about in this book. I had to look within, and beneath to find me again. I had to look through the window of my soul. I could not continue to go through the motion of life empty. I had to take back ownership of my life once more. Learning to find fulfilment, excitement, and enjoyment again, but as me. The real me. I wanted to live a life of being unapologetic, not owing anybody anything, and taking what I needed at that present moment in time. Most importantly, I needed to love myself first. To give the very essence of my being what it needed to be healed on all levels. I did just that and then the light broke through. It was like having an epiphany, a revelation.

At this present moment in time, I am at a place where I feel at one with myself. I surround myself with what I need when I need it. Whether it be peace, love, healing, whatever it is.

I can talk about my valley experience – that dark place for me, because I faced it and will always continue to have those moments as life is a process and a journey. I can only deal with what I can see and what I can acknowledge. I did not want it to become my truth, but it became my truth anyway. I took ownership of it and my faith helped me to stay grounded. I hope my experience and truth will be a light to someone who has either just visited that dark place or is looking to walk out of it.

I knew I had so much within me to offer, to myself first, and then to others. So many gifts lying dormant inside that had to surface. I knew someone out there was waiting for me. Waiting for my voice to add to theirs so we were amplified together. I owed that to myself first, but I also owed it to others not to stay silent and sit on my gifts and talents. To people I may never get the chance to meet personally, and countries I may never get to visit, I knew I needed to be true to myself always. I knew I had to get my voice out there, to be me and walk in the freedom of being me and make a difference with my life to fulfil my purpose and calling.

Goodbye Me, Hello Me was written from the heart and from a place that I had not visited before. A dark valley I had found myself in. It was birthed out of my own experiences and I am sharing my hurt, pain, and lessons with you. My desire is that you will be enlightened by this book, and it wakes you up to be *YOU* before it is too late. Allow this book to stir up something within you, to ignite a flame inside and awaken your passion for you to tell your own story, to live your own life, blaze your own trail, and use your gifts. You have your own life story to share if you choose to. Someone out there is waiting for you, so they can be set free. Your light needs to shine brightly again. So, give it the power it needs and let it shine! Find your freedom to be…

With Love,

Jennifer

Stand Out.
Be Different.

INTRODUCTION

Question:
What does the best version of you look like?

Is it about your image and the clothes that you wear? Is it about the material things that you have, and the exotic places you get to go on your vacation? Or, is it about self, and being your true form of who you are on the inside?

Everyone will have different answers to this question, and of course, we would, as we are all different, but what if I tell you that the best version of you comes from finding yourself and representing who you are at your core. It is one thing to have all the other stuff mentioned above, however, what joy is there in the appreciation of those things, if we do not enjoy being who we are?

Does this speak to you?

How often, at funerals, do we hear a eulogy of the person, and think it is more about their stuff (material) things than it is about them as a person? The lives they touched, the impact they made, and their legacy left behind. If they could take their things with them, I'm sure they would. We can spend our lifetime accumulating "stuff", that we forget to live. We forget to be ourselves naturally, and learn to love life, our life. In the midst of all this, we also forget most importantly, to love our self and to give our self what we need. To walk in peace, joy, happiness, love, forgiveness, and courage. We stop being our self, who we were created to be, and who we are at our core. Then, we adopt a lifestyle of what the world teaches and shows us how to live, and how to be and think, and what to say. Last time I checked, we are not robots and we are all not the same. If we do not watch ourselves closely, we'll find the world shaping and moulding us into its own image on how we should be. We are here to impact this world and leave a footprint, to make a mark. Not the other way around. I have seen personally, too many times, what can happen to individuals when the world has had its way with them and has chewed them up and spat them out. It is not pleasant, I assure you. I'm sure you know what I am talking about if you have experienced that for yourself, too, or know someone who has.

Goodbye Me, Hello Me is about learning to discover yourself again by letting go of the past and embracing the future. This book is about helping you to find *YOU* hidden within and pulling at the best version of yourself in the midst of all the chaos in life. In this book, I will take you on a journey to re-discovering yourself through keys to finding you. We'll be looking at where you are at this present moment, and how the past has impacted and influenced the now. How to break away from the place of stagnation, divorcing some things and some people along the way, and saying goodbye to yourself so you can say hello and welcome the new you. You will also learn how to make room for what is coming, while taking the time out that you need along your journey to just breathe and listen to yourself and your heart. The focus of this book is on the Mind, Soul, Body, and Spirit, receiving what you need for your tomorrow, by living today.

As individuals, we can get so caught up in our past, and planning for the future, that we forget the here and now, to live in the moment. Living and being in the moment, appreciating what we receive daily, believing it will sustain us for the day at hand, and having an attitude of gratitude. There is something about being grateful and giving thanks that frees us to embrace more in our life. More of yourself, more relationships, wealth, health, happiness, etc. We can be too focused on the end result - the destination, looking at getting it right and perfect, that we do not stop and think about the journey to that destination. How this journey is marking, shaping, teaching and moulding us, as we focus on our wellness, self-development, and spirituality.

Allow me the opportunity to walk with you on this journey, which I myself am taking, too. To walk with you through your metamorphosis, so you can gain your wings to fly again.

I hope this book will speak to you where you are at this present moment in time. Let this book act as a guide in helping you to discover more of who you are and fulfilling your destiny, by looking into the window of your soul.

You will be surprised to find what is hidden beneath.

Step Out And Be You!

ONE
WHERE IT ALL BEGINS

Understanding the moment

As with everything else, let's start at the beginning...

The world was formed; life was created, and we ruled the earth. Uhm . . . hold on just a moment! How far back do we need to go? How far back do you need to go? Is your beginning the dawn of creation? Is it from when life was begun? Is it from when your own life began at conception? Or is your beginning right now, on this very day, at this very moment?

We are all different—wired and created differently. We all begin uniquely—not at the same time or with the same things. What do I mean by this? Your beginning might be somebody else's middle, or their ending. What and how they started could be different from you. So, why do we still compare ourselves to everyone else, using a type of measuring stick? Then we view ourselves as inadequate and a failure in life. Can we really fail in our lives?

What makes you different is **Y.O.U** - Youthful, Original, and Unique. A prototype. No carbon copies. Just one of a kind.

Your beginning can be anytime, anywhere, and in any season. It is your beginning and no one else's. Your beginning can even reflect where you are right now, at this very moment. It is said we can all begin again and start all over. Many of us get many start-overs, which is okay. It does not mean that you have failed; it only means that you have been given another chance, another opportunity to try again. You are righting mistakes that you made wrong and trying a different way and approach. That's great, don't you think? It's not one strike and then you're out. Phew!

It is very easy to ask yourself, Why? "Why has this happened, or why has that happened to me?" We can also easily blame others for our lives and the choices we have made. Don't get me wrong, some things are out of our hands and control; however, most things that happen to us, we allow. Oops! Did I say that out loud? I will repeat it again. Most things that happen to us, we allow. Yes, you heard me. We give others consent to treat us in a way and manner that we do not see fit. We might not always give permission verbally, but through our physical actions and responses, yes, we do.

It is important for you to understand where you are at this present moment in time. Aware of what you are doing right now, how you are feeling, and who is around you. Pay close attention to your environment, and your community. Pay attention to how outside sources can affect you on the inside, and the person that you are, and the person that you were created to be.

You are going to look at the **SELF** first. Pay close attention to your feelings and emotions right now as they are letting you know what is happening on the inside of you. If you want to, you can write them down. You may decide to keep a journal or diary to reflect on as and when you need it.

Self-awareness is such a fascinating thing as it teaches us to not only acknowledge who we are as wonderful, beautiful human beings, but also to wake up! Wake up to the exciting, new possibilities that await us in life. How often do we get the chance and opportunity to take that in, and become aware of what is happening to us at that very moment? What is happening to our bodies as we continue to grow and develop physically, mentally, and spiritually? We can get so caught up with planning for the future, that we forget to live for the now. We forget to enjoy the day that we are in, and the step that we are on. We miss today by focusing too much on our tomorrow, and then we miss all the important things that are going on and taking place right now in our life. I'm not saying planning for tomorrow and the future is wrong, far from it. What I am saying is our tomorrow will not come or exist if we do not pay close attention to our today. From the decisions that we make, and our choices, to acknowledging our thoughts, feelings, and emotions. Look at the people we hang around with and allow them to speak into our lives. We can only ignore these things for so long until it begins to catch up with us and affect us on how we think and live our lives.

When we focus on our tomorrow, fear can quite easily rear its ugly head. What is **F.E.A.R**? False, Evidence, Appearing, Real. We then become overwhelmed, and it starts to affect us where we are right now, in this present moment. We are where we are right now because of choices and decisions that were made yesterday. Our past has affected our tomorrow, which is today. What choices are you going to make today - *present*, that will affect your tomorrow - *future*?

Through making the wrong choices and mistakes, our life takes a path we did not orchestrate or want to go down. But... life happens, or as others may say, "Sh*t happens". Yeah, it does. It happens to us all. However, it is what we do with that life which is important. What do you choose this day? To serve yourself first and put yourself first, or neglect you and put yourself much lower down the chain and serve everyone else – the whole world, before you? If you want to pour excellence into the lives of others, you must first pour that same spirit of excellence into yourself first and foremost. Just how important are you? Ask yourself these questions daily.

How important am I to myself?

How much do I mean to myself, my dreams, my ambitions, my family, my life?

Am I going to give myself a break and a chance at life?

Don't be hard on yourself. The world is an expert at doing that. Go easy on yourself, and do not beat yourself up. As long as you have breath, you have a chance. Live to fight another day, as they say. (I always wondered who "they" were). Make a note, whether mentally or written down, on where you are right now. Not only where you are, but how you are feeling. Your feelings and emotions are important. Do not ignore them. From there, you can begin to look at, and map out, what changes are required to make in your life right now for your tomorrow, for yourself first before others, i.e. Family, Friends, Co-Workers, Clients, etc. It is not selfish to think of yourself first. It is **SELFUL**. You need to serve yourself first with what you need before you can be in a position to serve others. You need to take what you need for yourself before you can give to others, to serve others with your presence before your presents, and serve with your gifts and talents. You cannot give what you do not have. Simple. So, being aware of where you are in the moment will help you to see what needs changing in your life. Then, the next goal is knowing how to through implementing steps, either by yourself, or you could work on that with someone, like a friend, counsellor, mentor, coach, etc. **Don't be too proud to ask for help when you need it!** Yes, I am speaking to you.

You are giving yourself the best chance in life when you can be real and be who you are at your core. Your DNA. Who you were created to be, and what you were created to do. You owe yourself that. No-one else owes you anything. The path you walk is *your* path. The shoes you walk in are *your* shoes. It is not one size fit all. Your life will look different, and be different from everyone else, and vice versa. It is not a sign of weakness to stop and take the time that you need right now at this very moment. It starts with you. You are seeking and desiring your life to mean something more again, and that can take starting again at the beginning, even reinventing yourself. So, the question again for you is…

Where is your beginning?

Chapter Highlights

❖ *Acknowledge where you are at this present moment in time.*

❖ *Make a note of the change needed internally and externally.*

❖ *It is not selfish to put you first. It is SELFUL.*

❖ *Don't compare yourself to others.*

❖ *Take what you need for yourself to help you to grow.*

Personal Thoughts

GOODBYE ME HELLO ME

Personal Thoughts

Believe In Yourself.

TWO
HELP, I'M STUCK

Moving on from where you are

How often do we hear the words "Help, I'm stuck"? When my youngest child was a toddler, sitting in his stroller, he would yell those words at me. I would look at him and sometimes laugh, as I found myself saying to him, "You are supposed to be in there, you are not stuck". My son did not understand that being restrained, restricted, and limited was for his best interest, as it kept him safe. Did you hear that? **It kept him safe**. How often in our lives do we view being stuck as something that is meant to keep us safe? Not often, I am sure. This is a place where we can take the time out that we need, even when we don't know that it is required.

Some of us think being stuck is a place of failure, that feeling of being immobilised, and not knowing what to do next, or where to go. When we find ourselves in "Stuck Valley", fear starts to creep in. We second-guess ourselves, our abilities, thought processes, and our life. Then, to make matters worse, we get our big ol' measuring stick out again, and start measuring up against others.

Have you ever thought that you were meant to be stuck for a reason and purpose?

That being in the valley may have something to teach you?

We are so quick to form judgments and think of everything negative about being where we are, that we forget that there could be a positive to be where we are as well. Like my child, like with every other child being strapped in their stroller, buggy, or pram, we sometimes get strapped and tied down to. We think it is because we have done something wrong that led us to this valley, or there is something wrong with us. Is there something wrong with you? Short answer, NO. There is absolutely nothing wrong with you. You see, "Stuck Valley", as I like to call it, can be a place of receiving what it is you need at that present moment in time, whether that is healing, a time out, reflection, re-focus, etc. It is a place and time to look at what is happening in your life at this present moment and seeing where you go from there. Life will throw you a curve ball from time to time. Being stuck can be something that intentionally makes you listen and wake up. It forces you to see it, and not ignore it. It wants you to listen to it, and to address it. Whatever your "it" is. That problem, issue or circumstance. I have always believed that being stuck was a bad thing. I don't know, maybe it was something programmed into my mind from when I was young, or from outside influences. However, I felt that there was something bad and wrong with me and saw that place as a punishment of some kind. Do you feel like that sometimes? We take on the blame game, and guess what? We become the victim. I'll say that again. **We become the victim.** The victim of life's circumstances. So, how can we turn this around? How can we move out of "Stuck Valley" with our bags packed, passport in hand, and ready to hit the road again?

You will need to look at where in your life at this present moment you have become stuck. Not only that, what happened in your past, your yesterday, that led you to be where you are right now in "Stuck Valley". This is not a blame game, rather, an opportunity being given to see what you can change, what you cannot change, and what you will accept, so you can move out and on with your life. This is your opportunity to shine a light on your life where there were none before. Nobody likes the feeling of being frozen and immobilised. One minute, you're driving down the freeway with the wind blowing through your hair, then the next, you come to a major stop sign, and to a halt. You can't go any further, and sometimes you don't know why.

So, what do you do?

Firstly, you are going to look at where you are now, and what is going on in your life today, your present moment. Remember, we spoke about this in the previous chapter. If you need to write this down, then do so. Look at, or list what tasks, jobs, whatever it is, that is going on right now in this very moment of your life. Don't forget to pay attention to your feelings and emotions as well. They play hand in hand in this and are very important. Acknowledging how you feel right now, and what emotions are running through you, will help you to understand your *why* for this present moment.

Secondly, take a look, but only a snapshot, of what has happened in your past that has led you to this point of being stuck. Again, you are looking at your actions, thoughts, feelings, and emotions. How far back into the past you go is up to you. However, be warned that whatever door you open, you need to be prepared to walk through!

Thirdly, you are going to look at what things, or people, you need to eliminate from your life right now at this very moment. Why go through the elimination process, you ask? You cannot move on from where you are and enter into your next season of tomorrow with baggage from yesterday. It is way too heavy for you to carry. So, you must begin the process of getting rid of some stuff, and I included people in this because sometimes that heavy weight can be people and not necessarily tasks that are going on in your life. It is one thing knowing you must carry yourself, but to carry everyone else with you on your back…that is a big, huge NO, NO. A tall order, if I may say so. You need to have a garage sale while you're in that valley. Think of it as a cleansing detox.

Do you remember what I said in the previous chapter about your shoes and one path that only you can walk on? You first must do you, before you can be present with others, connect with them, and serve them. You need to get rid of what is toxic in your life, right now in this present moment that is making you feel sick and ill, or is leading you to become stationary, or even stagnant. Sometimes, it can be us getting in our own way, or other people as well, so look at that option, too. You may need to show people in your life the door. Kindly, though.

Addressing those three nuggets right there will help you to look more closely with a magnifying glass at what is happening in your life right now that is causing you to become and feel stagnate, and, how to move on from "Stuck Valley". Remember, I mentioned the positive that can come out of being in that valley, too. Just like the example with my son in his stroller, sometimes being in that place is a way to keep you safe. Safe, protected, covered, and secured for a moment of time. It can be a place of time out for you to not only look at what is, and what is not working in your life, but also to take the time that you need out of your busy schedule to stop, re-evaluate, and take stock of where you are going, and the path you are on. It can also be a time for you to catch your breath and breathe. It is all about perspective, seeing a **negative turned back around to a positive.** What one person may see as an obstacle, barrier or hindrance; another person may see as an opportunity. My son was strapped in his stroller with a harness made to protect him to keep him safe, so he wouldn't fall out and injure himself, but also, so he could be transported around safely, easily and quickly.

Your "Stuckness" could be your harness. Your safe place, so you do not trip or fall. It could be where you need to be for a moment in time and season, so you can re-evaluate, reflect, plan, heal, or even grow. A time of looking and seeing what you need to take right now in your life. You cannot withdraw from you what has not been deposited in you in the first place. This may be a time to look at what is in your hand, and what you already have within you. We will get many of those "Stuck Valley" moments in life. Everyone! No-one is exempt, and we cannot escape it when it arrives. We must acknowledge it and allow it to do its process and work in our lives. The key is what you do while you're there, as well as how long you stay. Remember, life is full of lessons. Don't focus so much on the end destination, that you forget to live the journey to get there and to learn from those life lessons.

You are passing through the valley. How long you stay there depends on you. The intention is not to dwell there for so long that it becomes your norm. There are only so many times you can go around and around that mountain. It is very easy for mediocrity to set it, and then we become comfortable. Don't compare yourself and your journey to others. Everyone has their own path to walk on. Remember, it is not one shoe size fits all. If your feeling stuck right now, don't ignore it. Address it head-on, so you can continue on your path again, building yourself, and your tomorrow.

Chapter Highlights

❖ *There can be both positives and negatives to being stuck.*

❖ *It is not a sign of weakness or failure.*

❖ *You have another opportunity to make the necessary changes to your life. Take it!*

❖ *Look at what lessons are to be learned, so you can walk out of your valley experience.*

❖ *Keep the focus on YOU when you are in the valley.*

Personal Thoughts

GOODBYE ME HELLO ME

Personal Thoughts

Be The Best Version Of YOU.

THREE
GOODBYE

---
*Divorcing yourself,
and leaving the past behind*

Saying goodbye sounds so final. Finito. However, we need to say goodbye to the parts of ourselves and our lives that we cannot take with us into the next. Your next season, new life, a new chapter, whatever name you wish to give it. Goodbye is not just reserved for those areas of our lives and parts of ourselves we do not wish to take with us, sometimes you may have to wave goodbye to certain people in your life. People that are only temporary and there for a season, and people who you cannot take with you where you are going next on your journey. Saying goodbye can, for many individuals, feel like a period of grief, while they are experiencing the loss of something or someone, but, where there is a loss there is always a gain, even when we cannot see it, feel it or understand it. If we are going to make space for the new, we must give up something that is old. Something that no longer serves its purpose in our life anymore. Like the saying goes "Out with the old, in with the new".

What is this old you speak about; I hear you say?

Well, it can represent anything in your life that has run its course and no longer has the desired effect on you it once had. This could be:

- Changing a habit.
- Change of work or career.
- Expelling certain people from your life. You know the ones I'm talking about. The leeches, energy-suckers.
- Taking a closer look at your character and personality traits.
- Letting go of feelings and emotions that you have lived with, and dealt with for so long.
- Changing your geographical area i.e. moving home, country, etc.
- Decluttering your home.
- Plus, many more…

The old can represent anything in your life.

Another part of the process of saying goodbye could be through rejection. Being rejected by someone, especially if they are very close to you i.e. family or a partner. That is something you do not have control of as it is a decision made on behalf of someone else. Rejection can be a painful experience, but it does depend, of course, on how you look upon it from your own perspective. I have experienced rejection in my life many times, both personally and professionally, but the one area that has hurt the most, of course, for me is personal, especially when it is closer to home. You go through mixed emotions of not understanding the *why* and feeling as if it is your fault and you are to blame. I have felt that. However, I have also learned that I can only change my response and action to things, and how I allow it to affect me. I cannot change someone else's thinking if they do not want to change. That part, you will need to leave alone as it is out of your control. Whether it is you doing the releasing from your life or someone else, you are still saying goodbye.

The old that you are saying goodbye to can be absolutely anything that is halting and blocking you from progressing forward. This is something that must be addressed first before anything else. How can you focus on a clean slate with so much baggage in your life that you need to wave goodbye to? Baggage that you need to let go of. Baggage that weighs you down like a dumbbell around your neck. Remember, you are detoxing and decluttering here so you can move your life forward. You are making room for the more and the new. Getting rid of the old will allow you to do this, so you can start embracing the new.

Only get rid of the things that no longer serve its purpose in your life. Then rinse and repeat!

Looking at these points we just mentioned is the beginning of the shredding process, and this is where the next stage comes in…The Divorce.

Dictionary Definition -
Divorce: 1. A judicial declaration dissolving a marriage in whole or in part, especially one that releases the marriage partners from all matrimonial obligations. 2. Total separation: disunion. 3. To separate; cut off.

Once you know and list the areas that you feel need addressing for the elimination process, the divorce comes in. That separation cut off point that needs to occur in order to move forward into your next season. For many, divorce can be a horrible, emotional act that brings out all the past hurt, and pain because your wounds are open and exposed. You are in a vulnerable place. It is more about yourself than it is about the other person. It can be a place of loss and grief as I mentioned earlier. Sometimes it can be volatile.

For others, divorce could be seen as a time of celebration. Celebrating the cutting away of the old, freeing yourself, and releasing yourself for the new, exciting, and next adventure in life. Sometimes, people use this time to focus more on themselves. Their health, finances, career, and whatever else that need their attention right now, that they may have neglected in the past. They may feel like a weight has finally been lifted. I know in certain countries people have divorce parties and celebrations like it's their birthday. I remember a time walking into a card shop one day, and seeing a card that said, "Congratulations on Your Divorce" with a champagne bottle on it and a popped cork. Say what!! I could not believe it! I think these days we will celebrate anything.

I mentioned above about divorcing people, things and situations from your life that you have control of, but what happens when it is about you and you do not have control over it? What happens when you lose yourself? I hope this makes sense, but I will explain.

I have experienced loss in my life through death and losing things, whether through my own accord or through theft. However, the one thing I can say, is that the most painful loss I have experienced is the loss of myself. That is one of the reasons I am writing this book. When you have lost who you are, it is a terrible thing. You feel as if your identity, your message and your voice is silenced. You feel as if your vision and dreams, your inspiration, and source of light is diminished. You start to become tired, weary, drained and depleted that you just do not have enough energy to continue on. You look in the mirror and see your reflection and know it is you, but feel there is a disconnect from reality. You don't feel like yourself.

Sometimes people lose part of themselves but are not sure what part of themselves they have lost, but they know something is missing because they can sense it. They do not feel like themselves, as though there is a disconnection. The loss of myself felt so strong. I was grieving as if I had lost someone through death. It is like dying to yourself when you actually want to find the will to live and to fight on. It was a period of hurting and being in pain for me, but also a time of reflection and re-evaluating. I became numb to life as I was trying to protect myself and my heart from being hurt and wounded. I lost my sense of connectivity and my direction in life, as well as my sense of purpose. I wasn't operating at the full capacity of knowing who I was and who I could be at my core. It felt like my DNA was all messed up. This loss can be just as painful as experiencing any other loss in life. I was in that place for two years and trying to overcome so I could walk out of that darkness, that valley of the unknown, into a life that I so wanted and desired for myself, a life filled with freedom to be me.

So, why do some people welcome divorce, and others don't?

It is all about perspective and what is going on in your life at that present moment in time. Both the welcomers and non-welcomers of divorce can view it as a toxic and unpleasant time, however, how you handle and move on from it, has entirely to do with your perspective.

How does letting go of the past make you feel?

What emotions are you experiencing right now?

You want to get to the point where you are channelling and turning all of your built-up emotions, even your negative ones, into something positive that will help you to walk out from where you are whole and not broken. Yes, you may have to go through a period of healing and that is normal and to be expected. Allow yourself to be open to it and receive what you need at that moment in time. It's okay. You will be alright. What doesn't break you, will shape you.

Remember, this is about saying goodbye to areas of yourself and life that represent your past.

Your past does have a part in influencing your present because it is your story. It is the lessons, experiences, situations and mistakes that you had to go through, as well as your achievements you've accomplished along the way that has made you into the person that you are today, helping shape and mould you. However, your past does not define your future. Your past is your yesterday. Now, you will be focusing on your tomorrow, by acknowledging your today.

Dictionary Definition -
Goodbye: *Farewell: a conventional expression used at leave-taking or parting with people and at the loss or rejection of things or ideas.*

Are you longing for you to catch up to where your heart is? Ready to live a life that reflects who you are on the inside? Ready to be yourself, and not live a life of pretence? Just imagine… every day you get to be *YOU*. The real you, loving and accepting yourself for who you are. All the flaws, bells, and whistles included. None of us are perfect. Remember that! Perfectionism does not exist. It is okay to make mistakes, that is how we learn as human beings. It is an organic process. It is better to learn from mistakes, than not to grow at all through learning. When we become stagnant, that is when we stay stuck (remember "stuck valley") and live in the past.

Divorce yourself now and set yourself free. Find the freedom to be you. You deserve that for yourself and so much more. Do not settle in your life, go for the absolute best. Think of yourself more highly than you are. Not an in love with myself vanity way. There's a difference between loving yourself and being in love with yourself.

You want to be able to walk out and away from the old, so you can embrace the new. A new zeal and passion for life once again as the new you.

Chapter Highlights

❖ *What do you need to leave behind that you cannot take with you into your next season?*

❖ *Only get rid of the things that no longer serve their purpose in your life.*

❖ *Look at the baggage that are weighing you down.*

❖ *Allow yourself to be open to experience the new.*

❖ *Allow yourself to be open to receive what you need on all levels of healing.*

❖ *Remember who you are and don't you forget it!*

Personal Thoughts

GOODBYE ME HELLO ME

Personal Thoughts

*Live Free,
To Be You.*

FOUR
LOST PROPERTY

Getting back what is missing

Do you ever feel like you are riding the wave of life but recognising deep inside of you that something is missing?

You go through the motions of life telling yourself all is well, however, there is a knowing that something is missing. Something is not adding up in your life and you feel it so strongly. Your good at math but you know 2 + 2 does not equal 4 here. Something just doesn't feel right and you cannot put your finger on it. It does not make any sense. You definitely feel as if you have misplaced something that is so dear to you, precious, valuable and important. Your grieving but you just don't know why.

What is it? What's missing? What have you lost?

Answer… Yourself. You have lost *YOU*. Somewhere along life's highway, you have misplaced you. The things and beauty that make up who you are that brings light and life into your being, the love in your heart and the passion to your soul. Your light is dimming and fading rapidly, and you feel overshadowed and overwhelmed in this world. There is a sudden disconnect sometimes from reality. Your present, but you don't feel your presence. You feel lost and overlooked. Undervalued and unappreciated. You take a look in the mirror and you see yourself, but you don't see YOU. The reflection staring back seems different, somehow.

We spoke about losing yourself briefly in the previous chapter, and now we shall look at it in more depth.

It can be a terrible experience when something is missing, whether you lost it or it was taken or stolen from you. This could be a material thing, relationship, job, feeling, or even a loved one through death. It is like part of you has gone so now there is this empty feeling, a void that you are trying to fill. Be careful about what you use to fill that void in your life, it may not be good for you. You may find yourself going through a season and process of grieving and it feels so heavy like being pressured and weighed down. We all experience some kind of loss in life. No-one is exempt. However, what happens when it is you? What happens when you have lost part or all of who you are that you just don't recognise yourself anymore? You just about manage to live the best way you can but cannot shake off the feeling of being unhappy, incomplete, unsatisfied or unfulfilled. You have lost your sense of direction in life and find yourself in what appears to be in a very dark tunnel, scrabbling for the light to find your silver lining. Your spark has gone. Your countenance has fallen as you try to piece by piece your life back together like a jigsaw puzzle, but it just doesn't fit. Nothing works. The sizes are all wrong and the image does not connect no matter which way you turn it. You have lost your shazam!

Does this sound like you?

I have lost many things over the years, as I had mentioned before. Losing things from objects and opportunities, to close loved ones and relationships. I have found for me, that the greatest loss that I had felt was my loss of self. Losing yourself is like losing your presence, what makes you, *YOU*. It can be your character, personality, your passions and desires, visions and dreams, your heart and soul. It is what makes you connect with reality or your higher power that helps you to function and operate as you in this world. Losing yourself could also be your voice, but remember, your spirit can never be silenced.

Having experienced that kind of loss, you then start to disconnect from your surroundings. This for you could be your family, your relationships, work or career, community, etc. It can be anything that is or was of importance to you and your life. You try to discover the meaning of your existence in life, but find it is not making any sense at that moment in time, as your mind is not in that space or place of understanding.

This is where the danger could quietly and subtly creep in. You may start to adopt and entertain certain negative feelings and emotions that suddenly affect your behaviour and actions towards yourself and others. You may start to doubt and question yourself on why you are really here and what you are here on this earth to do. You may find that your self-esteem and confidence has been knocked, and you become saddened, disappointed and even angry with yourself and with your life. You may go through a period of rejection, therefore rejecting others around you, especially your loved ones. They are probably the ones you will reject first as they are closes to you, so you keep them at arm's length. You may find yourself slipping into a depression and find that you cannot function further than the day you are on. For some of you, you may start to entertain suicidal thoughts as you feel like you cannot continue with life anymore, and the only solution is to not be here.

You hurt when you lose yourself. You are in pain. Your soul hurts, your heart is broken, and if you're a spiritual person, you may find that there is a disconnect from your source. Not intentionally done, mind you. Just something that has happened. Losing you could feel like dying to yourself. Getting rid of the parts of you that need to be buried so you can be rebirthed and reborn, although we don't really seem to see it that way when we are heavily weighed down in the midst of it all, and are unable to see the light or bigger picture.

Brokenness can be so raw, real and naked. It can be like being stripped down to your bare necessities to rediscover, redevelop and restart yourself again, almost like giving you a jump start as you would a car battery that has died. You know the saying that people often say… "It feels like I have hit rock bottom and cannot go any further". Well, like the saying also goes… "Once you have reached rock bottom, the only way you can go is up!". Losing yourself can be looked upon differently by people, as it does depend on your own personal circumstances and perspectives. Some may look at it as a tough lesson to be learned. Some, as releasing of what is old and holding you back to receive the new. For some, it could be seeing it as something you have done wrong, so then it becomes your punishment.

You are not being punished or placed in the naughty corner!!

Saying goodbye is not just an external thing. Some of the life's lessons and the processes of life that we go through, much of it will be internal. It is about your being before your doing and re-evaluating yourself internally as well as outwardly. It is about getting yourself back to knowing, loving and understanding who you are, which starts with you and no-one else. How you are wired. How you think. What makes you tick. Who you are at your core. What you are destined to become in life. The greatest loss to life, to this world, and to others will be yourself. Whether you know it or not, you have so much beauty within you. You were created as a being of purpose, love and compassion. You have so many special gifts and qualities inside of you that need to be unleashed into this world. Your heart beats for what you are passionate about for yourself and life. We do go through life where we face so many difficult situations and circumstances that not only change who we are, but our course in life. That is part of life. We go through trials, obstacles and periods of testing. The ups and the downs. A walk through the valleys and around mountains. We become disconnected from ourselves, our visions, our dreams, and find ourselves "lost at sea". The key is to know how to find your navigation and reroute yourself back to dry land. To look beneath and within at your core to learn, love, know and understand who you are, whose you are (if you are spiritual), and where you are going in life. Your purpose and destiny lie within you and are connected to who you are.

There will be times in life when you will lose something. It can be anything. The key is to learn to recognise "it", and to discover it early so you can do something about it in time. If left untreated and neglected, it will become infected and will cause you more harm for your health and wellbeing. As I have mentioned so many times in this book, there is nothing wrong with taking that much needed rest and break for yourself. Your mind, body, soul and spirit need it. When we are thirsty, we drink. When your body is thirsting for something that is healthy to you, give it what it needs. Do not neglect yourself! You are too valuable and too precious to continue in life not living free to be yourself. Learn to put yourself first and serve yourself first. This is self-help. You cannot give what you do not have. It is that simple!

Chapter Highlights

••

❖ *Is there something missing from you and your life at this very moment?*

❖ *Discover what "it" is so you can address it in more detail.*

❖ *If you are experiencing a void within you, what are you filling it up with?*

❖ *Give your Mind, Body, Soul and Spirit what it needs. Do not neglect you!*

❖ *Take stock of the things and people that add or subtract from your life?*

••

Personal Thoughts

Personal Thoughts

You Are ONE Of A Kind.

FIVE
SILENCE

---
*Catch your breath,
and learn to breathe*

In life, you need to take moments to breathe... And I mean just breathe. You can get so caught up in life with the ups and downs and ins and outs, that you don't allow yourself time to catch your breath. When I was a child, I remember this advert with a toy bunny rabbit that would bang its drum all the time and kept on banging the drum, running around. The advert, of course, was promoting and selling long-lasting batteries, but how many of us feel like that rabbit? You keep running around, and sometimes in circles, banging your drum or head against the wall, and then you become so tired, depleted, and left with no energy. You think you have long-lasting batteries, but guess what? You don't! You need to learn how to find the time in your busy schedule to be quiet and just breathe. You need to re-charge your batteries, as they WILL run low on power if you don't.

Life can be such a battle, and an uphill one most of the time. You feel like you're fighting in a boxing ring most days, and you just about manage to get to your corner to replenish yourself with water and with what you need to go another round before you hear the bell - Ding, Ding!! This is all part of why it is important that you take a time out, and away, by yourself, from your busy life. Your body, mind, soul, and spirit will thank you for it. As I mentioned earlier in previous chapters, you cannot give yourself something that you do not have to give in the first place. You will constantly be drained until there is nothing left of you. You are no good to others or to life when this happens.

Learning to take a time out to breathe can happen in many ways…

- Exercise – Focus is on your health and your body.
- Meditation – Quiet your mind, soul, and spirit.
- Sole Activity – Reading a book, spa treatment, walking, music, etc.
- Time Out – Scheduling some time, even 10 minutes into your day to be still.
- Socialising – Getting together with friends and/or family.
- Holiday – Taking a vacation away from your normal environment.
- Plus, many more…

It is important to put yourself first for your own wellness sake. Do take note of areas in your life you feel need addressing so you can make room for a time out. Look at the things that need shifting, or even cancelling so you can get back the time that you need. When you forget your source – your connectivity and what gives you power, you lose your strength. When you forget who you are, you cannot function as you in this world.

Listen, you need time for yourself, with yourself and by yourself. This is something only you can do for yourself and no-one else. If you don't do this, your mental, spiritual, emotional, and physical wellbeing are in jeopardy. As human beings, we think we can function all the time at full speed and at 100%. Reality check…we can't. Simple as that. We were not built for that. We need to give ourselves time to recover before going again.

Example: A person comes out of the hospital after an operation. The doctor tells this person how important it is to rest and recover so their body can heal, or they will have a relapse.

What do you think would happen if that person does not take that doctor's advice, and just decides to go back to life in the fast lane? They would probably end up back in the hospital again, or even worse, would have done more damage to their body which would cause the healing process to take even longer.

When you take the time to breathe and be silent, you are healing yourself. To be **SILENT**, is to **LISTEN**. Both words have the same letters. You get that through rest.

REST = POWER

Don't become your illness. You must take the rest that you and your body needs. That is very important! There is so much power in silence. What is silence?

Dictionary Definition puts it like this…

Silence: ***1.*** *The condition or quality of being or keeping still and silent.* ***2.*** *The absence of sound; stillness.* ***3.*** *A period of time without speech or noise.* ***4.*** *Refusal or failure to speak out.* ***5.*** *To make silent or bring to silence: silenced the crowd with a gesture.*

A lot of people do not like silence. They find it very awkward, indeed. They feel like they need to do or say something to fill in the gaps of that silence. If you are not used to it, it can be hard to manage and do, however, it is possible with practice. How else do we get good at something if we do not practice, or learn the art or skill of doing that particular thing? There are some activities that incorporate silence like: yoga, prayer, meditation, and walking, to name a few. There is an activity I'm sure you can probably think of and can do that will work for you and fit around your schedule. Take the time to listen to yourself, especially in the moments of silence.

Your Heart – What is it saying?

Your Thoughts - What are you thinking about in this present moment?

Your Spirit – What are you feeling in this moment of connection with your higher power?

Your Soul – What are you discerning deep down within you? What stirs you or drives you?

Your Body – Are you in good health? What does your body need?

Pay attention to what is happening within you, as well as around you. You can get so focused on the outward i.e. your environment, that you miss what *YOU* need and what's going on inwardly. **You must take the time out to breathe as well as to listen.** I cannot stress that enough.

Let me ask you a couple of questions…

How many times in your life have you experienced burnout?

Has there been a time where one was far worse than the other? (i.e. it took longer for you to recover from it).

Burnout is not good. It can leave you feeling more tired physically, more drained mentally, your emotions can be all over the place, your health spirals out of control, and then you disconnect. Disconnection from life and from reality, struggling to stay grounded in the present. I know, as I have been there myself. Then before you know it, your doctor (if you have sought medical attention), is telling you that you're depressed, and pushing you some pills to make you feel better. You go into a slump. You feel immobilised. Remember that "Stuck Valley" place? You can't think beyond the day that you are on. You cannot move beyond the step you are on. You struggle to find the light in your situations. You struggle to find the air to breathe. You may even lie in bed all day, not wanting to wake up to face the day at hand. Does this speak to and resonate with you?

I will say it again. **You must take the time out to breathe and take the time that you need.** You owe that to yourself and to those around you. You owe it to your future self.

There is only one of you. That's it! That is what you get, and that is what everyone else gets. There are no duplicates or carbon copies of yourself. Just you. One of a kind. The original. That's it, amigos. If you do not look after yourself, then who will? Others may deem it to being selfish to think of yourself first, but it is **SELFUL** and not selfish. You must first serve yourself with what you need, so you can be present for everyone and everything else and give what you already have.

If this is your first time learning to be silent, start with 5 minutes of your day, and increase from there. You don't have to sit in silence for hours and hours, unless that is what you want and need. You'll probably end up falling asleep or turning the TV on or going on social media. Start with where you are and what you can manage for now and take it from there. Small steps at a time. Find some breathing exercises that you can do, if you feel that would help you to become still and quiet. If you are a person of faith, you might meditate or pray. Whatever works for you to help you to be still, quiet, silent, and just breathe. The stillness and silence are about quieting your soul. It's not just about quieting your surroundings.

You can do this! You've got this!

Chapter Highlights

❖ *Where in your life do you recognise the need to become silent?*

❖ *What ways can you be silent in your life?*

❖ *Take the rest that your mind, body, soul and spirit needs.*

❖ *Catch your breath and learn to breathe again.*

❖ *Look after yourself so you do not experience burnout.*

Personal Thoughts

Personal Thoughts

*You Are
A Gift To
This World.*

SIX
STOP, LOOK AND LISTEN

Looking within to find YOU

I remember as a child attending primary school, all the children had to learn how to cross the road properly and safely. The name of that campaign was called Stop, Look, and Listen (The Green Cross Code). It was to highlight where we were, where we wanted to go, and how to get there. It caused us to pay attention, to wake up and be aware of the dangers before and ahead of us. That is what so many of us in life need to do. Especially once in a while. Pay attention to ourselves and what is going on in our lives. To do that, we need to Stop, Look, and Listen.

STOP - Wherever you are in life. Grind to a halt.
LOOK - Within to find YOU. Where are you hiding at?
LISTEN - Be still and silent to hear what it is being said.

When you do these three things, it helps you to discover and learn more about yourself. The good, the bad, and yes, the ugly. You are not just looking at the positives, but the negatives also, and your strengths and weaknesses. How can you find yourself if you do not pay enough attention to yourself? How do you know where you are going in life if you do not take a time out occasionally to stop? If you were travelling somewhere and found yourself lost, wouldn't you stop and ask for help and directions?

We speak more than we realise. Speaking is not just limited to our mouths. We speak with our bodies, our actions, and our entire presence. We must learn to listen to ourselves and take note of what we are saying. This is also where the silence comes in that we spoke about in the previous chapter, being quiet enough to hear and listen.

Looking within to find yourself takes guts, I can tell you that. It takes stripping down naked, (not literally), becoming real and raw with yourself, and seeing *YOU* for the first time. To do this, you must look in the mirror. Look in the mirror to see what you see. Look within the window of your soul to see what you see. Will you like what you see? You must be honest with yourself if you are to live an abundant, fruitful life. You can lie to everyone around you, but you can never lie to yourself. You can hide from the world, but you can never hide from yourself, the person that you get to see and spend time with every single day of your life.

Let's break it down a little further…

Stop, look, and listen is like a traffic light system. The red acts as a warning for you to stop and become aware of the dangers of your surroundings. The amber is asking you to look again and the green is wakening you up to listen and put your feet to pedal, let's go!

STOP

Wherever you are right now in your life, and whatever you are doing, STOP. Now, when I mean stop, I am talking about taking a time out, putting certain things on hold, and not accepting any more workloads, invitations, friend requests (you know what I mean all those social media fanatics), etc. What you are doing is giving yourself permission to stop for a while, breathe, and take stock of where you are at present. When eating, before adding more food to your plate, you need to finish the meal you are eating first. You don't want to self-combust. Some of us live in a fast-paced world. A microwaveable world, hustling and bustling wanting everything yesterday, and we are lucky if we even know what day it is. We take on more than what we should, more than what we can handle, and we cannot say NO. Many of us haven't or even mastered the way to say it. We show up for everyone and everything, and hardly show up for ourselves when it matters most. We are consumed with society's way of accumulating more. More stuff, things, wealth, positions and titles, etc. However, we do not realise that we need to get rid of some "stuff" first before accepting more on our plate. But what about showing up for yourself?

How many of you have done a garage sale of some sort? Going through all the old junk and clutter to sell to make more room for…well, more things and maybe more junk. Things that you have hung onto and hoarded for many years telling yourself "Oh one day, I am going to need that". Will you?

Question: *If you had to suddenly go somewhere, never to return, and you had to take ONE packed suitcase in tow, what would you pack? What would you choose to carry with you?*

I find that having a lot of stuff can weigh you down mightily and heavily, that feeling that you are just treading water, and trying to keep your head afloat, but something just keeps on pulling you back down. It is even harder when you do not know what "it" is. This is where you need to STOP! When things become burdensome or overwhelming, and you do not know whether you are coming or going, just stop. Stop and breathe. We learn so much in the silence, then when we are at the height of the busyness that we find ourselves in daily. Once you can do this, and expect to do it quite often in life, you can then move on to the next step.

LOOK

How many times are we told to look up? "Look up and keep your chin up" our parents would say. That's all well and dandy, but what about learning to look within, too. You can learn a lot of things about yourself when you know how to look within. Where are you hiding at? You have so much to offer to this world. Yes, I am talking to you. You have hidden treasures on the inside, sparkly gems that are just waiting to shine in the world. How do you know what is within, if you do not look within? This is where holding a mirror to yourself is the key. What do you see when you look into the mirror? You pay attention to the outside of course, but what do you see when you look into your eyes? Are they etched with pain or discovery, or is there something else just waiting and anticipating for the right opportunity to birth itself out into the world? How do you feel in that moment when you're looking at yourself in the mirror? Do you feel ashamed, guilty, broken or embarrassed? Or do you feel love and acceptance? When you see yourself for the first time, what emotions are you feeling? What thoughts are running through your mind? Do you see another you waiting to burst out? Are you a different person, not the person you normally show others? Write down and make a note of everything in that very moment. That is your moment. Acknowledge it!

You can only work on what you can face. The mirror really has a way of revealing what you keep hidden, you need to know all of this. You are exposing yourself, not to the world, but to you first, only. You may feel vulnerable at that moment in time, naked, but you are trying to look within to find *YOU*. Look at your personality, your character, what makes you smile, laugh, and sad. Look at what tugs at your heart, wakes up your spirit and slaps you in your soul. You are stripping yourself bare so you can find *YOU* again. The real you. Who you are at your core? What makes you tick? Once you have looked at yourself under a microscope at all the little details, you can then move on to the third step.

LISTEN

The "YOU" that is hidden within, what is he/she saying? This is where you will need to listen, and I mean really listen to yourself. That still voice that is within crying to get out. You won't hear the cries if you are not positioned and able to listen. That place of quietness, stillness, and silence. You are quieting your soul to hear it speak. What is it saying to you? If the whole world ignores you, do not ignore yourself, too. If you feel like people don't listen, listen to yourself. It might sound silly, but really it works. You must pay attention to yourself. The answers you will find will be both positive and negative. You noticed I did not say positive *or* negative. You will get positive and negative answers as both areas are very important and must be addressed. It is like only focusing on your strengths and neglecting your weaknesses when both of them together make up who you are. You are just choosing what ones to focus on the more that's all, but do not disregard or neglect the other. Both are vitally important.

Be patient enough to hear the answer even when you do not like it. Listen to your heart. What is it speaking to you about? What can you hear? What are you feeling? I want you to be the very best version of yourself, and in order to do so, you need to pull the real you out. No carbon copies, just you. Be intentional and choose love over fear. Choose to love yourself first and foremost and operate from a place of love.

Through stopping, looking, and listening, you want to get to the point where you are acknowledging the real you on the inside, and show that side to the world. Show yourself off. You have so much to offer. Let your light shine, don't hide it away not to be seen again. Look at what is driving you from behind to propel you forward in life. Someone out there is waiting for your light. Someone out there is waiting for your gift and presence. Someone out there is waiting for the real you.

Can the real you stand up?

Chapter Highlights

❖ *Where in your life do you need to Stop, Look, and Listen?*

❖ *What is hidden on the inside that needs to come out?*

❖ *What is the driving force in your life?*

❖ *Learn to say NO. NO to yourself, and NO to others.*

❖ *Listen to what your heart is saying to you.*

❖ *Get real and naked with yourself.*

GOODBYE ME HELLO ME

Personal Thoughts

Personal Thoughts

You Are A Blessing.

SEVEN
BITE SIZE

Learning to walk again,
one step at a time

Watching a child walk for the first time is such an amazing experience. They first learn to crawl, and then before you know it, they are walking. The child does stumble of course in-between; however, they grow stronger and sturdier on their legs. That is the process of life that most children will go through. As a parent or caregiver, when we marvel and look at them, all we see is where they are at now…walking. We sometimes tend to forget the process of how they got there to that point, and what it took because we are just so glad they're walking. It is where most choose to focus their attention isn't it, on the end destination rather than on the journey itself to get there?

People often see us when we have made it, or when we are at the top of our game, so to speak, our peak. However, they do not know and see our humble beginnings. Where we came from, what it took for us to arrive at this point, and the process in-between. Just like a toddler learning to walk, we too are learning to walk. Learning to place one foot in front of the other and to hold our balance so we do not fall or stumble. However, there will be times, just like with a toddler, we will fall and stumble, and that is okay.

Do you give up? NO, you don't. You keep on going, doing the best you can, taking smaller steps and making progress. The key is that you are making progress. You are not where you have started. **You are making progress!**

We can sometimes get so focused on our end – setting goals, and the planning, that we forget to live the journey in-between. Focusing only on getting from point A to point B, that we don't pay close attention to what happens in the middle, the journey that is going to take us to where we are going. **We forget to live.** Don't let that be you. As human beings, we can get caught up in the hustle and bustle of life, and living in the fast lane, that we do not get to appreciate and take in the views along the way. Before we know it, life will pass us by, and we won't know where that time has gone, and you cannot get back. Let that not be you!

There will be times on your journey in life when you will fall and stumble, and that is okay. It does not bear any reflection on who you are as a person. It just proves that none of us are perfect. It is what happens after you take a tumble that counts. Do you just stay down and wait for the count of three and you're out? Or, do you rise up, dust yourself off, and go again? You have been given another opportunity, another chance to go again. The beauty of being given another opportunity is that you can begin again if you need to, changing what needs to be changed along the way and doing something different that you have never done before or tweaking what didn't work for you the first time. You will always have a blank canvas to work on. What you do with it, what masterpiece you produce and create is up to you. You are in control. You are designing your life. How beautiful it is, and the colours that you use, it is again up to you. No one has the right or permission to touch your canvas or create on it unless you have given away your right and permission to do so. What you put out; you attract. Remember that!

You are learning to walk again, taking one step at a time. Little bite size steps. No big chunks or leaps. Take the size of step that you can manage right now, for where you are right now in your life. Don't copy everyone else or their style. Just do you. You will have enough light for the step that you are on. Just focus on the day at hand, experiencing daily what you need to achieve what is required of you for that day. Just like a toddler learning to walk, when you have mastered the little steps, you can then move onto bigger steps. You have heard the saying right - "Don't run before you can learn how to walk"? There is nothing wrong with going, if need be, at a much slower pace than everyone else. Remember, it is not a race. You are not competing with everyone else, so you can stay in your own lane. Your focus and attention should be on you. Who you are, and what you are created to do. Not who you are in the eyes of others, and other people telling you how you should act, and what you should do. This journey is not about anyone else, it is all about you. So, take ownership of it. The pace you take in life is your pace and no one else's. Don't get your measuring stick out again, leave it be. You do not need to measure yourself up against anyone else. You don't need to because you are being you. Once you have mastered walking, you may feel like going for a jog first before running. You are focusing on your life and your journey. Where your finish line is, is something determined by you and not by others. Don't compare your finish line to everyone else. Remember what we covered before in previous chapters, your beginning could be someone else's middle or end.

So, do not compare yourself to others.

How do you learn to walk slowly, taking bite-sized steps?

1. Look at where you are right now, at this very moment. What are you doing? How are you feeling? Who do you have around you? Etc.
2. Manage what you have on your plate right now or learn to get rid of stuff that no longer serves its purpose in your life. Ask yourself, Is it fruitful to me? Is it of benefit and adding to my life? Or is it draining me, subtracting, and leaving me lifeless? Be ruthless. You are not a hoarder or a walk-in closet.
3. Once you have looked at, cut off, and re-evaluate where you are at present, it is time to get walking. You are learning to walk again, by taking smaller steps for now. You cannot focus on the big steps just yet. Small is best. You will build up to taking

much bigger strides when and where necessary. You'll know when you are ready for such a huge step. Wait. Be patient. Take your time.
4. Break your day or time into little bite sized tasks that you can focus on and manage. You do not want to give yourself a headache! If that means stripping your day down from doing twenty things to ten, do what you need to do. The key here is not to be overwhelmed with what you must do, and with where you are.
5. When you have mastered those tasks, celebrate! You must find the time to celebrate you. If you don't, then who will? Celebrate when a task is completed. Celebrate what you have achieved. Be your biggest and best cheerleader. Poms poms and all!
6. Reward yourself. Learn to treat yourself when you have accomplished something good. Go out with friends, loved ones, or take yourself out on a date. Something nice, and special for yourself.

Treat yourself. You deserve it!

Take small steps at a time. Once you have built up balance, stamina, and confidence, you can increase the size of your steps. Before you know it, you will go from walking to jogging, to running, in no time. Even when you are running at full speed, like we spoke about in previous chapters, learn to take time out to stop, breathe, and rest. Your mind, body, soul, and spirit will thank you for it. You are looking to make progress in your life, but heed this; **Don't confuse**

movement with progress. It's not just about what you have. It is about what you do with what you have.

What happens if a baby or toddler eats too quickly? Or if they try to run too fast before they have mastered walking? They can cause damage to themselves and their bodies. You do not want that to happen to you. Take what you need for where you are at present, going along with bite size steps if need be. Take in the journey around you, so you can make the necessary adjustments along the way as, and when they arise. You do not want to go speeding along, because before you know it, you have gone through a red light, and have a speeding ticket in your hand. Go slow. If that is what you need right now, it is okay. Do not apologise to anyone for being you, and for taking what you need right now. Have you heard the story about the tortoise and the hare? Speed does not always win the race!

We can spend so much of our lives running around like headless chickens and throwing spaghetti at the wall to see which ones stick, that we miss one important thing. We miss us, our own self, in the process of life. We miss loving ourselves, valuing, respecting, honouring, and appreciating ourselves, and speaking life into ourselves. We need it. People are not always going to be around to encourage you, so you will need to learn how to encourage yourself sometimes. Look to celebrating your milestones. Celebrate your wonderful gift(s) to this world. Celebrate you.

I'm championing you and cheering you on.

Chapter Highlights

❖ *What areas in your life do you need to take bite size steps in?*

❖ *What life masterpiece do you want to create with the blank canvas that you have?*

❖ *Remember, it is not a race. Go at your own pace. Stay in your own lane.*

❖ *Manage with what you have, and with where you are right now.*

Personal Thoughts

GOODBYE ME HELLO ME

Personal Thoughts

Use Your Voice.

EIGHT
LET'S GO!

Planning for success

So, let's do a quick recap...

- You have understood the moment of where you are at present. Looking at where everything begins in your life.
- You have acknowledged where and how to get help from being un-stuck and moving on from where you are.
- You have said your goodbye's and now are looking to leave the past behind you.
- You have discovered it is *YOU* that has gone M.I.A (missing in action), and looking to find yourself again.
- You have learned the importance of catching your breath and embracing silence in your life.

- You have woken up to find *YOU* hidden within, through stopping, looking, and listening.
- You are experiencing walking again, taking little bite-size steps as you go, and managing with what is comfortable for you.

Now that you have done all of these steps, you can move unto the next step… Planning for Success.

What is success? What does success mean to you?

Dictionary definition puts it like this… *Success: 1. The accomplishment of an aim or purpose. 2. Favourable or desired outcome. 3. The attainment of fame, wealth, or social status. 4. One that succeeds.*

Success can mean different things to different people. There is no right or wrong answer, it is your interpretation of what success is, and what it means to you. For some, it is about wealth and position. For others, it could be family and health. There are really no right or wrong answers here. Whatever your definition of success is, you are going to be planning for it. You attract in life what your heart desires and what you put out.

What does your heart seek after?

What do you crave for in life?

For you to know how to get to where you would like to be, you need to plan. Think of it as ordering your steps. You get to visualise, dream, and see what your life could be. What you desire and what is in your heart. What drives you, and what is burning passionately deep within your soul. You are getting the opportunity to create. You have a blank canvas to work with so… GO BIG! Don't let your dreams limit you to what you want to do and be. Think big out of the box. **No Limits. No Boundaries.**

Right, let's create!

What could you do if you had the opportunity?

Where would you go?

Who will you serve with your unique gifts and talents?

When would you like to achieve this?

What will this look like?

You can do all the planning in the world, but without action, your plans will just stay as plans. Your dreams will stay as dreams, your visions as visions, and your gifts will go unused, unnoticed, and unvalued. Planning for your dreams is important. Dreams without a goal plan are just dreams. Have you heard the saying "You don't plan to fail; you fail to plan"? To achieve your goals, you must apply discipline and consistency every day, even in life's difficult moments. You have to work at it, taking your bite-size steps if you need to.

Where to start? At the beginning of course.

If you have gone through the other chapters with a fine-tooth comb and held a magnifying glass to your life, you will have something to start with now. Unless your way ahead of me and already know what you want, which is great! We are going to take one thing. Just one thing at a time. You don't want to be overwhelmed. You can apply this practice to pretty much everything else in your life, tweaking as and where necessary as you go.

You are going to start with the ONE thing you would like to focus on the most right now. It can be anything you want. It can be something external like a job or career, to something internal to do with yourself. You might start with a pain that you have, or an experience that you went through in life which is giving you the opportunity to birth something new to help serve others with your knowledge, lessons, wisdom or gift. Whatever it is, give your pain a purpose. Don't let it die. You can start with anything you like. Don't forget, you're creating here. You have a blank canvas.

Whatever you have chosen to focus on right now in your life, you are going to write it down so you have "it" in front of you at all times. It is important to have that dream, that vision in front of you that you can see every day. You need to be constantly reminded of that goal.

When you write down that dream, vision or goal, you are going to write down your **WHY**. Why? Because it is your *why* that will keep that dream alive for you. It is and will be the reason that you are doing it in the first place. It is something that will keep you going during the times you feel like giving up, times of difficulties, or when you feel inadequate to fulfil that dream and that vision. You can write it down anywhere you will be constantly reminded. Put it on your noticeboard, in your phone or calendar, journal, a post-it note on your mirror, paint it on your wall if you want. Just get that dream, that vision, in front of you daily.

Next, you are going to visualise having achieved that dream and goal. There is something about when a person visualises, you tap into a part of you that knows no limitations or boundaries, just like when you were a child and you felt like you could do anything and be anything. You want to adopt that childlike faith again when you are visualising your dreams. Your dreams can be big and endless, and sometimes may not make any sense to others, but it is your dream. It's not about anyone else anyway. If your dream makes sense to you, that is all that matters. When everyone around you may think you're going crazy (and that will happen sometimes), see yourself walking in that dream, experiencing it, taking it in, and feeling it. What does the dream look like to you? Make a note of what you see and how you feel. This is where you're allowed to let your imagination run loose, remember as children. Write it all down.

The next step is for you to look at where you are now (in the present moment), to where you would like to be (your tomorrow-future), and plan how to get there. This is taking your dreams and visions and manifesting them, so it becomes real and tangible. I am talking about strategizing here and setting goals to achieve that dream and vision. This is where the bite-size steps will come in. You are taking your steps, one at a time that will take you forward towards that vision. This is where you put action to your thoughts and giving it a purpose. That is your ultimate goal. What those steps could look like depends on what your dream is.

Let's use an example of starting a new venture.

Peter wants to serve his community by starting a small group or organisation. His vision is to help the young people in his neighbourhood who do not have any place to go in terms of out of school activities, or youth programmes to keep them occupied and off the streets and teach them how to be adults in this world. This is where, at one point, Peter had found himself in life when he was younger. He visualises seeing every young person coming through his programme receiving the help that is needed to help build them up into strong citizens and world changers. But how? Where should he start?

First, Peter is going to do some research on what places, centres or opportunities currently exist in the neighbourhood and community, who they cater to and what services they offer. If there is nothing, then Peter has found his niche and a great place to start building. He will need to research how to start a group or organisation as well. Peter may decide to do some courses or training to help him learn to get where he wants to go. Peter will also need to conduct market research through surveys and interviewing both adults and young people alike, to see what they feel is needed in the area, and what help they need personally, and the challenges they are experiencing. This will show Peter what solutions he can provide to solve the current needs and problems experienced within the community.

Find the problem, provide the solution.

Do you see what is happening? Peter is starting to lay the foundation and build up a picture of what is needed for himself and others, so he knows how to help others and what steps to put in place to achieve his goal – his dream. He saw a map in his mind of his vision and that is guiding his footsteps on his journey to completion. The world is not just about supply and demand. You are plugging a gap by bringing what you have to those who are in need and can really thrive and benefit from it. It is about asking yourself how you can be a help to those around you.

Peter is then going to take all that research and start mapping out a plan of action to get him from where he is now to where he needs to be, so he can start to help those young people and families in the local community. The focus here is on the goals that will be set, daily and weekly goals that will get Peter one step further to achieving that dream. Bite-size steps, remember? As well as mapping out goals to do in the interim, Peter will be mapping out what he wants his first year to look like, maybe up to where he sees himself in five years' time, and beyond. This is focusing on your mid-level to long-term goals.

Your goals should be firm but not set in stone. The reason for this is because life can change at any minute. We live in a world where not everything goes according to plan and things keep on evolving. You will need to take a flexible approach here, an organic approach. Allow things to happen and lead you freely. Don't force it. You never know where your life will take you, and you will need to be flexible and adaptable to it where necessary. Don't be rigid. Even when painting a masterpiece, an artist can make mistakes and get things wrong, but will leave space and time to correct it to still produce something spectacular. Things may not always go according to plan; however, it will take time and patience to fulfil it and if you stay the course with your planning for success, you will get there. At the end of all that planning, the end goal is for Peter to be living that dream he visualised months, or years ago. What Peter did here was he turned a painful time in his life into a happy time and he is now positioned to give back. He gave his pain a purpose.

The above was just an example of what can once be viewed as a negative, turned into a positive. The key here is to plan by strategizing and setting goals to achieve the desired outcome that you are seeking. There will be highs and lows, but keep going and stay the course. Don't you quit! You don't want to be an empty shell with everything going great on the outside, and nothing on the inside. It will not bring you happiness. You do not want to destroy yourself on the way to success. It is not worth it!

Whether it be a job or career, business, family, or self-development, whatever it is and whatever your building, think ahead, think above, think within, and plan for success.

Chapter Highlights

❖ *What passion will you follow, that you will never have to work another day in your life?*

❖ *What is your soul crying out for, that will never leave you alone?*

❖ *Put action to your dreams, and your goals.*

❖ *Keep your WHY in front of you at all times.*

❖ *Give your pain a PURPOSE.*

❖ *Define what success means to you and plan for it!*

Personal Thoughts

GOODBYE ME HELLO ME

Personal Thoughts

Find Your Smile Again.

NINE
SAY HELLO

Embracing the new you

There is such freedom when you say goodbye to things that have run its course in your life and say hello to embracing the new. What you have done over the course of the previous chapters is acknowledge where you are at right now in life and what you are carrying, and learning to get rid of what's holding you back so you can be released. You are making space for the "new" in your life. Just like children grow from babies to adolescents, they get to experience everything new for the first time, and you will, too!

You are shifting your mindset and thinking from the old and the negative to the new and the positive. This is a new season for you. A new season to walk, live, find your smile and to laugh again. A new season of loving yourself, walking in love and experiencing that love for yourself. It's about taking the new you into whatever you have planned and envisioned for yourself and your life. It is about being who you are at your core, your real self. No fakeness. No pretence. Just you.

This is a time to adopt new habits, if need be. To adopt new approaches, and to make the right and necessary changes to your life, no matter how painful. This is a time to be open in your being, your vessel, and to be at one with the universe and embrace all the wonderful, beautiful, unique gifts and qualities that make up who you are. Learning to stay true to yourself, your core and DNA. It is about carrying you into the present with your presence and allowing it to speak. It is about allowing your gifts to make room for you.

When you are at one with yourself, with your higher being and power, and with your calling, you will begin to walk into your purpose. Knowing why you were created, and for what purpose. Adopt an attitude of gratitude. Saying "thank you" in advance for what is already yours and continuing to be in place of thanksgiving and praise.

What are your expectations in life?

Do you wish to do better, and expect to do better?

The focus of the new you should be on the mind, body, soul, and spirit. Coming into alignment with who you are, as your soul transcend time, space, and matter. Stepping out with confidence and boldness, knowing you can do anything. You can have anything you want (within reason). You just have to claim it! The only thing that will stop you from receiving is *YOU*.

The only thing that stands in your way is you, so learn to get out of your own way.

You are not always going to get it right, and life is about taking chances, leaps, and risks. You will never know what you can fully accomplish here on this earth if you do not try. We sometimes question if we will fail. Well, what if you didn't fail, and you succeeded? Also, there is nothing wrong with failure. See it as another chance and opportunity being given to try again, start again, and put right what went wrong. It is a learning curve and something that must be seen as a positive more than a negative. That is something that I had learnt for myself. The world is waiting for your gifts and your talents. Don't let it go to the wasteland. I remember hearing something years ago, and a question was posed, "Where is the richest place on this planet?". Of course, people were naming so many places from countries to continents, but do you know what the answer was?

The answer was the cemetery. Did you catch that? The cemetery. Why is it the richest place on earth? Because so many people die with untapped and unrealised potential. They die with their dreams, visions, and goals not being fulfilled. They die with inventions in them that the world will never get the chance to see or experience. That is thought-provoking, isn't it?

Let that not be you. Let us not die without having the chance and the opportunity to fulfil what we were put on this earth to do. Someone out there is waiting for your gift. Someone out there is waiting for your invention to make their life better. Someone is waiting for your presence to bring light into their lives. Someone is waiting for *YOU*!

Step into your **CALLING**. Walk in your **PURPOSE**. Say hello to yourself by embracing the new you.

If the new you consist of looking at yourself physically, maybe focus on your health and fitness level. If it is your family, and not having enough time with them, look to see where you can make time. If it is dropping certain people that surround you, do so. You will find that what is to come, the replacement, will be far better, uplifting, and enriching for you than what has gone, that has left you feeling depleted and dry. New people and connections will compliment you and add to your life, they will not take a piece out of it. It is like having a nice sweet dessert made to your liking, to your specifications. Then, someone comes along with a big ol' knife and take a big piece from out of it. That person is meant to add to your dessert to make it even better, like with sprinkles or cherries on top, and not take a huge slice from out of it. That is not adding, that is subtracting!

If it is looking at your job or career, are you destined to create something new and build your own business? To be your own boss or move up the career ladder? There are so many areas you could look at in your life, but whatever you choose, wherever you decide to put your time and focus, be you in the process. Don't settle for second best, and definitely, do not compromise on being you.

You may find you are surrounded by people that do not like the new you, and the changes you have made to your life. There is nothing wrong with you. Maybe they cannot handle the new person that you have become and the brightness of your light. The new person that was always waiting to come out from the inside but didn't know how to. Sometimes there are people that cannot handle your giftedness, potential, or your strength. It does not bear any reflection on you, remember that. We cannot please everyone and trust me; someone will get disappointed or left behind. That's how life works. You cannot take everyone with you on your journey. Not everyone is meant to go with you. When embracing and walking in the new you, you will find that your circle of friends and connections will change, and maybe get smaller. You'll begin to notice that the people you surround yourself with now are there to edify you, and not tear you down in order to make themselves feel good. Those negative ones are the people you do not want around you. They are the reminders of the old you, and who you were before in your yesterday. They are the people that won't be able to handle who you are now and where you are going. That my friend, is part of the divorcing period we spoke about in earlier chapters.

You are saying hello to yourself, to your life, and to the new you. Welcome yourself once again. Embrace yourself. Love yourself. Treat yourself with kindness. Be that shining light to yourself and to this world. Be that example. Someone out there is in need of what you have. Don't cover it up. Don't bury it. Don't hide it under a bush. Let your light shine. The world is waiting for you!

Chapter Highlights

❖ *What space in your life do you need to make room for the new?*

❖ *What do you need to wave goodbye to, so you can say hello to?*

❖ *What do you expect from life?*

❖ *The only thing that stands in your way is YOU.*

❖ *Get rid of what holds you down and holds you back. Release and let go.*

❖ *Get ready for what is to come...Hello!*

Personal Thoughts

Personal Thoughts

Live Life With Purpose.

TEN
RECAP!

Summary

Congratulations on making it to this chapter. I hope this book has spoken directly to your soul and awakened it, and you have started to take some action in stepping into the new you. I know it can be difficult when it comes to evaluating yourself on where you are now, how you are feeling and what your next step will be. In this last chapter, we will run through and do a recap of the previous chapters covered in the book. At the end of the chapter, I will suggest what types of further help and support are available so you can receive the help required with life's journey of discovering you again.

Chapter One Where It All Begins – *Understanding the moment*

In this chapter, we looked at where your beginning was by understanding your here and now, your present moment in life and being aware of how important it is to look after and put yourself first before anything and anyone else. How your life today has been decided by decisions made yesterday, and by changing your thought processes today will help impact and transform your future. There is nothing wrong with starting again at the beginning, if you feel that is what you need right now in life. Just decide on where your start-over point will be and work from there. Don't be afraid to give yourself what you need when you need it. You are too valuable to continue in neglecting you!

Chapter Two Help, I'm Stuck – *Moving on from where you are*

In this chapter, we looked at what it truly meant to be stuck and helpless. We explored the benefits of being in "stuck valley", and to view it another way as something adding to your life and not just taken away. We looked at how you can begin the process of preparing for your "moving day" from your past into your future. This valley experience is again another opportunity for you to evaluate past hurt, pain and decisions that have led you to be there, and how you can walk out of that dark place. This is your time and moment of reflection and release.

Chapter Three Goodbye – *Divorcing yourself, and leaving the past behind*

This chapter delved further into the specific things that you needed to wave goodbye to and show the exit. These were the areas of your life whether objects, emotions, opportunities or people, that had overstayed their welcome and the eviction notice had to be served. We looked at what it meant to go through a period of divorce so you can leave the past behind. Sometimes getting rid of things can be hard, as you can be holding on to the very things that need to be separated from you before entering your new land of freedom. Things that can bring ill health to you, but because you don't see it, you feel as if it is good, right and healthy. This was and still is your opportunity to re-evaluate and take stock of your life so you can be in a position to move forward, being the very best version of yourself.

Chapter Four Lost Property – *Getting back what is missing*

In this chapter we explored the meaning of losing something of significance to you, and how to get it back. We looked into what "it" could mean to you, but also discovered that a big part of losing yourself is *YOU*. Everything that makes up who you are is missing, and you are trying to discover it again so you can find your way home. When it comes to lost property, some things can be replaced. However, there are some things that just cannot be replaced, and you are one of them. You are irreplaceable. An original. One of a kind. That is why we spoke about how important it is to find you again, hidden amongst all the hurt, pain and circumstances of life. You owe it to yourself not to neglect who you are anymore, but to learn how to tap into, nurture and develop who you are so you can continue on life's journey again free to be *YOU*.

Chapter Five Silence – *Catch your breath and learn to breathe*

With all the busyness around us in life, it is not often we allow ourselves to take moments out to just breathe. This is what we learned and discovered more of in this chapter. How important it is to set aside time to be silent and catch your breath for the next step and journey you are to make in life, to give what your body needs which is rest. We looked at the many different ways you could do this i.e. activities, and understanding the importance of allowing your mind, soul and spirit to disconnect from outside sources for a while so you can regain your strength and power again. If you are to continue in life as the real you, bringing silence into it will help you to recognise when you need to withdraw and catch your breath.

Chapter Six Stop, Look and Listen –*Looking within to find YOU*

In this chapter, we looked at how important it was for you to stop, look and listen to yourself and pay attention to what was being said. It is your compass to help you to find your way and navigate through life. This starts with looking within to discover who you are, to find the real you. This can get lost with all the commotions of life. To focus on more of what you want in life, you will need to be present with yourself at all times. Your being is just as important as your doing, if not more. Discovering you allows a freedom to express who you are at your core, and be all that you were created to be and do in life. It starts with you!

Chapter Seven Bite Size – *Learning to walk again, one step at a time*

We looked at learning to walk again in chapter seven. Learning to walk one step at a time by taking manageable steps for you and your life. Running your race fast will not always mean you will win the race! Do not compare yourself to others. You are making your own progress and going at the speed that is right for you. While you are learning to walk again, we looked at the different areas of your life where you could free up space, time and movement so you could step out and away from the old into the new. It takes boldness, strength, confidence and courage to learn to walk again after being knocked down by life. Learn to take what you need when you need it. This is part of the process of you walking out whole.

Chapter Eight Let's Go! - *Planning for success*

This chapter was a big one for us. We talked about getting behind the driving seat and what that may look like in your life. When you get rid of something, you will need to look at what you might replace it with. This is where the planning came in where you were thinking about your successes in life and how you want it to look. We looked at how to find your passions in life. What this may look like. How to find your "WHY", and to dream again. You want to give your pain a purpose, and give your life meaning. Use your time of tests and trials and let it be a testimony and help to others. You cannot separate your visions and dreams from you. It is part of who you are at your core. Think about and plan how you want your life to look and feel, and then put action to that plan. Give it life while you discover *your* life again and walk into your destiny, calling and future with a purpose.

Chapter Nine Say Hello – *Embracing the new you*

For you to say hello and welcome something new, there had to be something you had to give up that was old and not healthy for you. In this chapter, we looked at how to welcome and accept the new you by embracing all of who you are. You learned the importance of getting out of your own way, so you can walk in your purpose and calling in life. You have said your goodbyes so you can say hello to the new you that was always within. It just needed some help in being exposed, first to you, and then to others. This is your new land of promise and opportunities. What you do with it is up to you. How you cultivate that land is up to you. Your continual growth and development are important if you are to attain what is yours and multiply. Have faith and believe in yourself that anything is possible. Welcome to the new you!

You have learned to identify where your faults are, what and who was holding you back, as well as the emotions and feelings expressed that was hindering your progress and breakthrough. You also learned how to bring closure to your life by saying your goodbyes, and allowing yourself to be open saying hello to the new you. I applaud you for making such a huge, brave step, and I can't imagine it was easy.

If you would like to take that extra step and go the extra mile forward with further help and support for your life's journey, there are places, people and things you can do to help move your life in the direction you want.

Some of us are strong in dealing with life changes by ourselves, which is great. For some, they may find that extra support is required.

1. If you are looking for one-to-one help and support, I would recommend speaking and working with a counsellor, listening ear, coach or mentor. It depends, of course, on what your needs are. You may find it more comfortable speaking with someone close to you and who you know personally if you think that will help you.
2. There are small groups that exist where you can receive help collectively with other like-minded individuals who are in the same situation as you, and where you can learn from one another. This may be something you can access physically or virtually, to suit your availability and needs.
3. You may be someone who loves to read a lot and therefore can find numerous self-help, motivational, and self-development books on the market either online or in bookstores.
4. There are also courses, trainings and programmes you could take to help learn more about you and

what you would like to do with your life, providing you with the tools, knowledge and resources that you need.

The possibilities are endless and there is help out there if you go seeking for it. Just ensure it is the right help and support that you need for where you are in life.

If you are someone who has read this book and would like to continue in learning and discovering more about yourself with me, I have teachings, courses and programmes that could help you. There is an E-Course that accompanies this book to further help discover life again as you. It is called **Goodbye Me, Hello Me E-course**. To learn more about this course, you can visit my website at **www.jvmwilliams.com** for more information. If you would like to connect with me online, you can find me on Facebook, YouTube, Instagram and Twitter @jvmwilliams.

Love Yourself, Always.

CONCLUSION

And finally...

We can all get lost sometimes on our pathway in life. We come across many crossroads on our journey, obstacles, hindrances and barriers. It is how we overcome them and move forward with our self-intact which is the important thing, even when sometimes we don't always know how to.

Starting again does not have to mean at the bottom, necessarily. It could be just starting over where you are, or where you last left things off. Your focus should not just be on what you are building around you, but also what you are building within you. You are strengthening yourself at your core, so you can carry on, walking your journey taking the time out that you need along the way and listening to yourself. This is vitally important. You cannot continue to go through life like you are being dragged kicking and screaming. You have to take back control of your life once again, from the choices that you make daily, to your decisions which steer and guides your course in life. From the people you allow around you, the work that you do, to the way that you feel. You are only in this world but for a moment. Make that moment count. Leave a legacy behind that you will always be remembered for. Don't exist just to exist, and then you're gone. Exist to live. Live your life with boldness, tenacity, confidence, excitement, and to make a difference in this world. Walk your truth. Live in service to humanity.

Release what is dead and buried inside of you. Take another look at the people cluttering up your life that you need to clear and get rid of. Ask yourself, "Do these people contribute to me in any way?". "Are they enriching my life?". Be upfront with people by telling them what you want and need. Don't presume that they will know. You must speak up for yourself. Don't stay silent. Know how to let things go so you can grow and thrive. Let it go so you don't block the flow. If it no longer serves its purpose in your life, then release it.

Replace fear with love and be disciplined enough and intentional to always choose to operate in love. Love yourself, always. Take care of yourself and make yourself the number one priority in your life. Do not neglect who you are. Build up your confidence, self-esteem, self-value and worth. This is your time and season to soar. Manifest your greatness. Be a high achiever and an overcomer. Show up and show out in your life. Get something out of it. Take ownership of your life once again. Allow yourself to be open and free to experience the new. The brand new **YOU** that awaits that you have always desired. You will always spend your lifetime learning, so be teachable. Do not act like you are a "know it all". No one likes that.

Be present. Be present with yourself first, your higher power, and then to those around you. When we turn on a tap, we expect water to come out. What will flow out of you when you are turned on? Will it be clean or dirty? Will it be wholesome, or make others sick? Will it speak life and healing, or bring death and disease?

You Decide!

No one should be dictating your life. You are in control. Take the wheel, reinvent yourself and see where life will take you. It may not be a straight road from A to B and life is not always like this, but you will still arrive at your destination refilled, refuelled, refreshed, restored, and revived. Your journey will be filled with scenic views, landscapes, and valleys, but you will come out stronger, more developed, refined, and ready to experience the beauty of life again with acceleration, impartation and manifestation. It is not going to be easy, absolutely not. However, it will be worth it. There is nothing more in life than just being you. Releasing yourself to be you and walking in the footsteps and freedom of being you. Enjoying life again as you, loving as you and receiving the rewards of life as you.

Think highly of yourself. Stay true to who you are. You are a precious pearl, a gem, so do not cast or through it away idly. Treasure and value everything that makes up who you are. You were born to sparkle!

Let's sparkle together!

Personal Thoughts

GOODBYE ME HELLO ME

Personal Thoughts

Personal Thoughts

GOODBYE ME HELLO ME

Personal Thoughts

Personal Thoughts

Personal Thoughts

Personal Thoughts

GOODBYE ME HELLO ME

Personal Thoughts

ABOUT THE AUTHOR

Jennifer V M Williams is an Author, Mentor, Speaker, Counsellor, and Coach. Her heartfelt passion is to see people be all they are created to be, and to help equip them with what they need to transform their lives and future. She is the author of **The Power of Your Thoughts** – 15 tips to help overcome the battle in your mind, and her newest book out now, **Goodbye Me, Hello Me** – A journey of discovering and finding yourself again to live the best version of you. Jennifer also has another new book in the works which will be released in 2020. As a Transformational Listener and Coach based in the United Kingdom, Jennifer is committed to using the pain, experiences, lessons, and challenges of her past to reach out to others and be a lifeline.

Jennifer does not just draw from her work and life experiences alone to help people, but also knowledge, training and skills learnt over the years in Business, Counselling and Psychotherapy, Psychology, Coaching and Mentoring, to name a few. With clients she has worked with worldwide, it has always been her main focus and goal to see individuals be set free to create the life their way, and to live their fullest potential. To connect and learn more about Jennifer, you can contact her at the following details:

Jennifer V M Williams
Kemp House
152 -160 City Road
London, EC1V 2NX
England
United Kingdom
Website: www.jvmwilliams.com
Email: support@jvmwilliams.com

GOODBYE ME, HELLO ME E-COURSE

Are you looking to go forward with the next chapter of your life's story?

If you have enjoyed reading this book, and would like to go just a little bit further in helping you to release the old and welcome the new in your life, The Goodbye Me, Hello Me E-Course is available for you today.

You will be taken on a three-week journey of **Awakening**, **Shifting**, and **Advancing** your life even more, in discovering the best version of YOU. This is your time and moment right now, to make the decision on the life and future you desire to have.

To find out more, visit www.jvmwilliams.com for information.

The next decision you make is your first step in saying hello to a brand-new life as YOU.

www.ingramcontent.com/pod-product-compliance
Lightning Source LLC
LaVergne TN
LVHW011949070526
838202LV00054B/4865